Pickles for
Breakfast

By Carolyn Soto Jackson

Published by:

Little Oaks

Little Oaks Publishing
www.thepublishedword.com

ISBN: 978-1-964665-23-8

DEDICATION

This book is dedicated to my sweet
nephew, Gabriel.

Happy birthday mijo, I love you so much.

This book belongs to:

_____

In an old, red barn lived
thirteen best friends.

Though they all looked different, they loved one another like family.

Pickles the pig loved rolling in mud, often splattering Blink, the white rabbit who lived nearby.

On the other side, Belle the clumsy cow, with a heart-shaped spot on her nose, jingled her golden bell as she wandered where she shouldn't.

Next came the four funny fowls—Honk the goose, Mrs. Crackers the sassy duck, Pepper the chicken, and Rusty the rooster, who woke everyone up with his "Cock-a-doodle-doo!"

Nibbles the donkey, recently moved, was learning to be gentle after accidentally biting Sassy the sheep and Gertie the goat.

In the small feed room, Rascal the
raccoon snoozed all day,

often startled by sneaky Fin the fox.

At the end of the barn stood Soccerball, a majestic white horse with black hooves. He was the barn's wise and loving counselor, always helping friends make peace.

One stormy morning, the farmer brought extra treats—
crisp radishes, tender eggplant, and crunchy carrots.

But the leaky roof meant the food would get wet!

Working together, the animals hurried to gather everything into a safe, dry pile. But where was Fin?

Suddenly, Fin popped out of the pile, his fur covered in smashed bananas and spinach. Apple slices peeked from his teeth.

"Where did you get those apples?" asked Pickles.

"I found them!" Fin lied, though he had taken them before the farmer could share.

"Those were for everyone. Please give them back," Pickles said kindly.

But Fin scoffed, "If I do, can we have Pickles for breakfast?"

Pickles' heart sank, and tears welled in her
eyes. The animals gasped

Then, Soccerball stepped forward and said,

"Fin, you must apologize. Your friends love you."

Fin turned his nose up. "I didn't do anything wrong. If you don't give me all the treats, I'll leave and never come back!"

"As you wish," said Soccerball, his voice gentle. "But we love you and don't want you to go."

Fin huffed, shot a glare at his friends, and stomped into the dark, rainy woods.

The animals were heartbroken. They left their treats behind and prayed for Fin.

One by one, they shared how much they loved him.

Hiding nearby, Fin overheard. He felt ashamed but refused to admit he was wrong.

"They're just tattletales," he muttered, blinking away tears.

For three days, Fin wandered the cold, wet woods. Hungry and lonely, he thought about his friends. He realized they weren't tattletales, they cared about him.

He even remembered how Pickles always saved peanuts
just for him.

Finally, he knew what he had to do.

Soaking wet and with his tail tucked low, Fin returned to the barn, unsure if his friends would forgive him.

To his surprise, they came running.

"Welcome home, Fin! We've missed you!" they cheered,
wrapping him in warm hugs.

Fin smiled "I'm sorry," he said "Can you forgive me?"

"Of course!" Pickles shouted "We love you."

From that day on, everyone was in hog heaven. Fin learned that true friends always forgive, and that honesty and kindness make a barn feel like home.

THE END.

www.ingramcontent.com/pod-product-compliance
Lightning Source LLC
Chambersburg PA
CBHW041633040426

42447CB00019B/3482